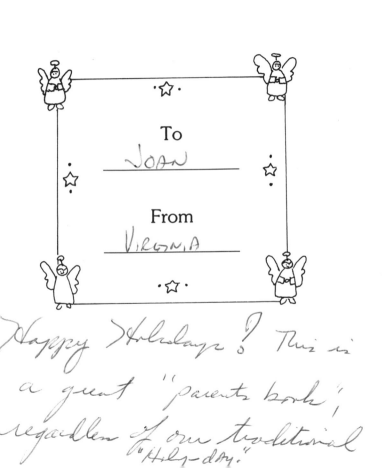

To

JOAN

From

VIRGINIA

Happy Holidays! This is
a great "parents book",
regardless of our traditional
"Holy-day".

OTHER BOOKS ABOUT EVERYDAY LIFE
BY DAVID HELLER

Grandparents Are Made for Hugging

Fathers Are Like Elephants
Because They're the Biggest Ones Around
(But They Still Are Pretty Gentle Underneath)

My Mother Is the Best Gift I Ever Got

Love Is Like a Crayon
Because It Comes in All Colors

"Growing Up Isn't Hard
to Do If You Start Out as a Kid"

Mr. President, Why Don't You Paint Your
White House Another Color!

Dear God: Children's Letters to God

Dear God, What Religion Were
the Dinosaurs?

The Children's God

The Best Christmas Presents Are Presents Are Wrapped in Heaven

"If Jesus was here right now, he would have friends that were Christian and Jewish and Moslem and Chinese and others too. We should remember that."

Hannah, age 10

The Best Christmas Presents Are Wrapped in Heaven

Children on Christmas

David Heller

Elizabeth Heller

Villard Books   New York 1993

Library of Congress Cataloging-in-Publication Data
Heller, David.
The best Christmas presents are wrapped in heaven: children on
Christmas/David Heller and Elizabeth Heller.
p.   cm.
ISBN 0-679-41760-5
1. Christmas.   2. Children—Quotations.   I. Heller, Elizabeth.
II. Title.
GT4985.H345   1993
394.2′68282—dc20   93-3475

Manufactured in the United States of America on acid-free paper.

9 8 7 6 5 4 3 2

First Edition

To our dear friends:
Lucille King,
for her kindness and
the religious spirit she
brought to our wedding ceremony,
and to Dan and Gail Connolly,
for their support, love, and friendship.

Introduction

Christmas is a season of the heart, but some people say it's hard to find Christmas underneath all the wrappings. Who better to lend a lighthearted and thoughtful perspective to this sometimes paradoxical time of year than children? After all, when a day of busy holiday baking, crowded malls, and shopping sprees has ended, children can quickly remind us where the heart of the Christmas season lies: in the spirit of giving and sharing. Their clever comments and inspired insights often seem heaven-sent.

Children are the link between material gifts and God. Sure, they're eager to imagine what Santa Claus might bring them, but they tell us that God has a "wish list" too. This list starts with loving each other and ends with loving each other.

Children also observe things about Christmas adults can easily miss during the rush of preparations. They might make certain a carrot is left for Rudolph along with Santa's cookies, or even more poignantly, they might stop to place a Christmas quarter in a homeless man's hat. Children are family oriented too. They seem to know instinctively that Christmas is also about sledding down a snow-covered hill with your family, and then retiring to the warmth of the family hearth with a cup of hot chocolate.

When all is said and done, the holiday itself is really about birth and childlike wonder and a sense of renewed promise about life—all of which our children represent to us. During the Christmas season, we hope that you will take time to laugh and reflect. Through the children's precious thoughts and witticisms about Christmas, may you discover much joy and even a little Eternity.

—DAVID AND ELIZABETH HELLER

The Best Christmas Presents Are Wrapped in Heaven

Reflections on That
Special Holiday Called Christmas

"Christmas is like a big surprise party that God
gave the world."

Henry, age 9

"Everything sparkles at Christmas . . . especially
the people."

Stacy, age 8

"Christmas is the day when all the toys from heaven get shipped down here."
May, age 9

"It was when Jesus was born and a lot of reindeer got jobs because they needed animals that could travel fast, so people would know about it."

Evie, age 6

"It's the only time in the year when it's okay to try to get fat. . . . It brings you closer to Santa Claus."

Joey, age 8

"Christmas helps you to remember other people, like the poor. It tells you that they like to get cans for presents."

Polly, age 7

"Some people say that Christmas is too expensive, but I don't agree with them. . . . You can say prayers for free."

Kersten, age 10

"I like the way angels got used like mailmen in those days."
Lane, age 9

What Is Your Favorite Part
of the Christmas Story?

"When Rudolph learned to have more faith."
Taylor, age 6

"How Jesus got born even though all the hotels
were full or cost too much."
Johnny, age 7

"I like how the three kings brought presents and that
gave Santa Claus the big idea."
Guy, age 7

"How the shepherds got some time off
from their jobs."
Paul, age 8

"It was real good how there was a big star in the sky
so they could see the roads at night while they
traveled. . . . We could use that star now
for the highways."
Nancy, age 9

"The best thing is how everybody realized that the
birth of a child is a very important thing
for the world."
Russell, age 10

The Strange Behavior of Adults During the Yuletide Season

"It's like magic. They stop rushing around and they stop screaming. Some scientist should study it."
Faith, age 10

"A lot of adults got big secrets then, but we figure it all out on Christmas morning."
Greg, age 7

"I seen them kiss more at that time of year."
Sammy, age 6

"Personally, I think they spend too much money on the colored light bulbs."

Dennis, age 9

"They like to go to parties and drink eggnog and act like the rest of the year is just how they pass the time on their clocks."

Gary, age 9

"They put out soft candies where even a kid can reach them."

Brian age 6

"They're happier because they got Jesus on their minds."

Michael, age 6

What Mom and Dad Say
About Christmas

"Oh no, here comes Christmas. . . . My poor wallet!"

Damon, age 10

"Be nice to Santa Claus when we get to the mall.
He might have a headache by the time
he gets to you."

William, age 7

"I remember one Christmas when we didn't get a lot of presents because we couldn't afford it. But it was still a good Christmas, because our cousins didn't get much either."

Guy, age 7

"We used to be happy to just get one present. . . . Oh, the good ol' days!"

Gordie, age 8

"There are Christmas angels all around, but some people can't see them. So, children, you should act like angels to help those people out."

Marie, age 8

On How Christmas
and Chanukah Are Alike

"Both holidays help the candlemakers stay busy."
Shari, age 9

"Chanukah is for Chanukah people and Christmas is
for Christmas people, but God is for all the people."
Crystal, age 7

"They're similar because the Jewish parents and the Christian parents both get exhausted by the time it's all over."
Richard, age 9

"They are both holidays about wise men who know a good miracle when they see one."
Kevin, age 10

"The holidays are connected if you are a Christian, since Christmas is supposed to remind you that your ancestors were once Jewish too."
Matthew, age 9

"Both of them show you how God is the answer to a lot of problems in the world. He fixes things."
Carey, age 7

"Chanukah has eight days, and Christmas is really supposed to have twelve days, if you believe the words to that partridge song."

Coleman, age 9

"They are God's holidays. God likes to get all kinds of mushy prayers from everybody then."

Arnold, age 10

"They both have stars as symbols of love. . . . Then it changes to hearts in February."

Anna, age 8

On Why the Holidays Are Good for a Family

"Christmas makes families say 'God bless you' even
when nobody sneezes."
Brandi, age 10

"Families need a rest from work and school, and
they might need to go skiing too."
Cindy, age 9

"Working hard together to bake Christmas cookies and put frosting on them builds up your characters in the family."

Marie, age 8

"It shows you that you can be a happy family even if you live in a manger."

Lem, age 10

"It makes the parents happy to see their children act like angels and sheep that don't talk . . . in the Christmas pageant."

Marianne, age 9

"Christmas is the one day that you can wake everybody up
and get away with it."
Gaye, age 9

How Is Santa Claus Different From Other Grown-ups?

"Santa Claus only buys the *best* stuff in toy stores."
Dale, age 8

"No different. He has a weight problem too."
Mo, age 6

"Santa Claus just deals with good children, and most parents have to deal with all kinds."
Elise, age 8

"He really gets to talk direct to God. He ain't fakin' it."

Henry, age 9

"Santa Claus has to work on Christmas Eve, and the rest of the people just take it easy and loaf around."

Amy, age 6

"He gets along good with people from all different religions . . . not just his own."

Kelly, age 9

"He says 'ho, ho, ho.'. . . The regular adults just say 'no, no, no.' "

John J., age 9

" 'Tis the Season To . . ."

"Write your congressman and demand that Jesus
gets another holiday too."
Larry, age 10

" 'Tis the season to be named Holly."
Holly, age 10

"Around Christmas time, my mom acts real sneaky, like she's got something to hide. So we start looking for it and it's usually under the bed."

Janice age 10

"To kiss under the mistletoe. . . . But it's okay to be choosy about who you kiss."

Yvette, age 8

" 'Tis the season to have loving thoughts in your heart and Christmas cookies in your stomach."

Victor, age 10

"To forget your worries and leave them up to God to help you with them."

Kersten, age 10

" 'Tis the season to be a child at heart."

Sylvia, age 10

What Is the Surest Sign
That Christmas Is Coming?

"You hear people whistling 'Jingle Bells' and nobody
cares if they whistle good."

Adam, age 8

"Grown-ups start to panic because it's getting late
and they don't have their shopping done."

Matthew, age 9

"You get the feeling that a lot of surprises are coming your way."

Carey, age 7

"The biggest sign is one that we can't see. God is busier than before. He's working on what people really need for presents during the year. . . . All of the best Christmas presents are wrapped in heaven . . . then we get them later on."

Sylvia, age 10

"During Christmas you could paint all of the big office
buildings in the world bright red and bright green."
Trent, age 8

Christmas Cards to God

Dear God,
Merry Christmas. Do unto others like you would
have them do. So let us have a longer vacation from
school at Christmastime.
Thanks,
Adam, age 8

To God,
Happy holidays. Merry Christmas. Happy Chanukah.
Do you celebrate them all?
I bet it's more fun that way.

Sean J., age 8

Dear God,
Could you send me some skates? If you're out of
your office, could you have an angel take care of it?
Merry Christmas

Lynn, age 8

Dear Jesus,
Happy birthday and merry Christmas. I guess it's all
the same to you.
Love,

Lori, age 7

Dear God,
You are the best God a kid could have.
And the only one too."
Merry Xmas,
Henry, age 9

A Card for God,
I don't draw reindeer and Santa Claus too good but
I believe in you a lot. I figured that would
matter more to you.
Kersten, age 10

Christmas Cards From God

Dear Children of the World,
Merry Christmas. You're my favorite people. But the
rest of the people are okay too.
Love,
God

Holly, age 10

"Christmas is a holiday that comes with its own music."
Kersten, age 10

Hey, Kids,
Have a *groovy* holiday. I talk this old-fashioned way
because I'm old.
God

Sylvia, age 10

To all of the countries,
Don't give up on peace. It takes time. I didn't create
the world in a day either.
I wish you peace,
God

Marianne, age 9

Dear People,
Christmas trees are pretty, but maybe you should be
a little better about saving some of those trees.
Holiday greetings,
God

Joan, age 10

Dear Children,
I'm giving Jesus new sandals this year, but don't tell him because it's a surprise.
Merry Christmas.
God

Ross, age 10

To the World,
Happy holidays! Here is something you should know: Don't worry so much about me getting real mad at you or things like that. You need to get to know me better."
God

Sylvia, age 10

How the Tradition of Having a Christmas Tree First Got Started

"Trees were on sale in the Holy Land."
Marshall, age 9

"Trees are a symbol of growing. . . . When Jesus was born, the world began to grow up."
Holly, age 10

"Maybe some little tree needed a home."
Evie, age 6

"Santa Claus used to hang trimmings on the reindeers' antlers, but the reindeers complained because it gave them sinus troubles. So trees was the next choice."
Kelly, age 9

"The trees got roots and so do we. . . . We got roots in our teeth, and we got the kind that God started with all the religious grandfathers."
Trent, age 8

How Does Santa Claus Really Find Out If You've Been Naughty or Nice?

"He knows people in the government."
Keith, age 10

"His wife has women's intuition . . . same as my mother does."
Louise, age 10

"Santa has one guy that is in charge of naughty and one guy that is in charge of nice, so he doesn't do all the work by himself."

Jonathan, age 6

"He has a giant satellite dish up there at the North Pole, so his communications system is pretty good."
Craig, age 9

"Santa Claus hires a friendly spy who does an interview with your parents."
Dick, age 7

"Santa Claus can predict the future. Like he knew when the economy was going to get rotten. So he bought his toys ahead of time."
Adam, age 8

The First Questions Santa Claus
Asks Prospective Elves

"What kind of flight insurance do you have?"
Keith, age 10

"Can you make chocolate that looks like me?"
Carey, age 7

"When does Santa take vacation? Does he go to the
beach in Florida?"
Jasper, age 6

"So you want to be an elf, huh? You boys don't have a big hang-up about making dolls, do you?"
Nancy, age 9

"Do you know the words to 'The Twelve Days of Christmas'? Can you sing on key?"
Marianne, age 9

"Are any of you prejudiced? Good, you're not. Because I'm going to have you working with some blue elves, and I won't stand for any meanness."
Serena, age 8

"Do you elf candidates love children? That's the most important thing of all."
C. Allan, age 7

" 'Twas the Night Before Christmas and All Through the House . . ."

"You could hear my father snoring."
Ross, age 10

"All was quiet except for some stirring mouse that was wrapping Christmas gifts for the mouse children."
Carey, age 7

"Nobody could sleep because the Christmas lights from the neighbor's Christmas house were too bright."
Gordie, age 8

"Kids were cheating and looking at the presents."
Andi, age 8

" 'Twas the night before Christmas and God was sure glad to have tomorrow off."
Sylvia, age 10

About What Santa Claus Thinks When He Sees Milk and Cookies Left for Him

"I hope those are *diet* cookies."
Cory, age 8

"Food? They always leave me food. Who needs more food? I'm fat as it is. Why don't they leave me a Red Sox cap? They're hard to get at the North Pole."
Norm, age 9

"Christmas makes you dream about all kinds of things . . .
and if you behave good and you're lucky, a lot
of them will come true."
James, age 10

"Oh no, not this family again. The father always eats the chocolate chip cookies before I can even get here."
Michael, age 6

"I appreciate this food because God doesn't let me take any breaks tonight. That God is a tough boss, but actually I love the guy."
Coleman, age 9

"How thoughtful of these nice folks. . . . You know, people really are good at heart."
Kersten, age 10

Behind-the-Scenes Questions the Children Would Like to Ask Santa

"How do you transport big toys like pool tables? . . .
You must need a flying truck for them."
Robbie, age 8

"Santa Claus, do you know the Bible by heart?"
Marie, age 8

"Santa, are you hiring elves for next year? Everyone says I'm short, so I bet I'd make a good one!"
Kirby, age 9

"What do you do the rest of the year? Are you an executive or something?"

Charles, age 8

"Do you have any children? Will they take over when you retire?"

Andi, age 8

"Are you getting tired of the same old red suit? I would be if I was you."

Thomas, age 7

"Santa Claus, are you immortal? How did you get picked for that?"

Brendan, age 7

The Significance of the Words "Silent Night" in the Famous Christmas Song

"Finally, no more noisy people crowdin' the stores."
Lindsay, age 8

"It's supposed to be a quiet night because back there in the Holy Land, Jesus needed his sleep to get ready to do the miracles."
Gaye, age 9

"It's a song they started singing to get the kids to be quiet. They were noisy because they were excited."
Dean, age 8

"It means that peace is a good thing and it might even be a holy thing, if it lasts long enough."
Richard, age 9

"When you see somebody special being born, you get kind of amazed and quiet."
Matthew, age 9

"It snows on Christmas when they have some snow to
spare in heaven."
Marie, age 8

On What Determines Whether It's a White Christmas in a Given Year

"If there were any wars in the world that year, then God doesn't let it snow."

Jan, age 9

"Maybe the angel that's in charge of snow gets its signals crossed sometimes."

Paula, age 8

"God doesn't want to spoil us, so he
keeps us guessing."
Damon, age 10

"The weatherman might have something to do with
it. . . . It might be his fault."
Bernie, age 6

How Do You Think God Spends Christmas Day?

"He watches *Miracle on 34th Street*."
Lyle, age 10

"It must be a day of rest because I think he likes those days of rest."
Nicholas, age 8

"He plays cloudball. . . . It's like football, but you throw a cloud instead."
Ken, age 10

"He goes to a big Christmas party and tries to find a date in Heaven for New Year's."

Arnold, age 10

"A lot of the time, He has to find out what went wrong with the big snow machine."

Robbie, age 8

"He says prayers to Himself . . . but that gives Him a headache after a while, and so He goes and visits with some grandmas and grandpas that came up to Him in the last few weeks."

Terry, age 9

"He attends a big graduation ceremony where some of the angels get their wings."

Anita, age 9

"If it's a He, He carves up the Christmas turkey. But if it's a She, then She sets the table and She takes a nap because She did all of the shopping and wrapping for Christmas."

Lauren, age 8

"It's the happiest day of the year for Him because His first son was born on that day and parents always like to remember things like that."

Colleen, age 8

"God just relaxes and starts planning some miracles for the coming year."

Carey, age 7

"God goes to a place like the White Mountains and sits around the big fireplace and rests. God doesn't need to eat, so God just takes in all the love from around the world."

Marcus, age 8

If You Could Give a
Christmas Present to the World,
What Would It Be?

"I would give the world more people who know how
to make you laugh."

Robin, age 8

"I don't know. It would be hard to find a candy cane
that was big enough for all the people of the world."

Mo, age 6

"I would try to bring Jesus back as soon as
he had the time."
Christopher, age 8

"I would promise to get rid of all the thiefs in the
world, or maybe try to reform them."
Donnie, age 9

"I wish the people of the world more free time to get
to know each other and understand each
other better."
Stacy, age 8

"I would wish everybody a merry Christmas and
then I would pass out candy to all of the little
ones and then I would pass out money to
all the big ones."
Rhonda, age 10

Special Personal Wishes
for Christmas

"That we could all be nice all year long, not just
at Christmas."
Nicole, age 8

"I wish I could eat all the holiday goodies I'd like to
and not get fat."
Marianne, age 9

"I wish the world had more playgrounds and I could visit them all."

Melissa, age 6

"I wish God wouldn't be so shy, and I wish he would come out and say hello to me."

Helena, age 6

"I wish that Christmas would only be over when the children of the world say it's over. Then it would go on forever."

Shelly, age 9

"My wish is to know a lot about Christmas because I would feel very proud to be in a book about Christmas."

Drew, age 8

What Is the Real Message
of Christmas?

"You should love people. They're nice once you
get to know them."
Joy, age 7

"Life ain't bad. It's good. Honest, it is."
Jack, age 8

"Peace on earth, goodwill to men, and better
manners for the men too."
Yvette, age 8

"Giving beats being a Scrooge, at least nine times out of ten. Well, maybe ten out of ten."
Ross, age 10

"Jesus was born in a manger and it turned out okay. If you have to stay in a bad motel, it's okay. You shouldn't be ashamed."
Sylvia, age 10

"The message is that wonderful things can happen here on earth too . . . but most of it starts higher up."
Henry, age 9

"You can have Christmas even if you don't have a fireplace and chimney. . . . All you have to have is a family."
Alice, age 9

How Can We Include Every Person in the World in the Spirit of Christmas?

"We should build a Christmas tree the size of the Statue of Liberty and put one in every country."

Gaye, age 9

"Let's rent some airplanes and have them drop Christmas gifts in all the poor countries."

John B., age 10

"Give every person a cupcake shaped like a friendly snowman that says on it: YOU'RE INVITED TO CHRISTMAS."
Lindsay, age 8

"Have a giant Christmas party with food from all over the world and make sure all different kinds of people are invited."
Carey, age 7

"The whole world should try to hold hands at once, and some lucky person might find out that they were holding God's hands."
Janet, age 10

The Many Reasons
That Christmas Is Beloved

"The food is yummy! Stomachs love Christmas for
that reason alone."
Robbie, age 8

"It gives you a chance to think about other people
for a change."
Carey, age 7

"It's a neat story how one kid's birth started
the whole thing."
Brett, age 9

"Christmas makes everyone have a bigger heart."
Marie, age 8

"It is something you can count on every year . . .
because it's created so it doesn't ever go away. . . .
It's forever."
Art, age 9

"It's all about hope . . . hope for your family and
hope for all of the rest of the families around too."
Kelly, age 9

ABOUT THE AUTHORS

DR. DAVID HELLER is a leading authority on children and their views of religion and the world. He has authored a number of successful books on the subject, including *Love Is Like a Crayon Because It Comes in All Colors*, *Talking to Your Child About God*, *Dear God: Children's Letters to God*, *The Children's God*, and *"Growing Up Isn't Hard to Do If You Start Out as a Kid."* His work with children has been featured all across the country, including segments on *20/20* and CNBC, and articles in *People*, *Parents*, *Good Housekeeping*, *Redbook*, *USA Today*, *Psychology Today*, *Parenting*, and in nationally syndicated pieces for Universal Press Syndicate. He graduated from Harvard and the University of Michigan, and has taught at both as well.

ELIZABETH HELLER, M.S., has assisted on all the previously mentioned books and has co-authored *Grandparents Are Made for Hugging*. She has developed a children's news program for cable TV and produced and hosted a radio show for children on WBZ in Boston. As Director of Public Relations for Catholic Charities, she did considerable work for children and children's charities. She holds a bachelor's degree in English from Santa Clara and a master's degree in journalism from Boston University.